BILL
GATES

Microsoft Founder and Philanthropist

by Marylou Morano Kjelle

Content Consultant
Anthony Rotolo, Professor
S. I. Newhouse School of Public Communications
Syracuse University

Core Library

An Imprint of Abdo Publishing
www.abdopublishing.com

www.abdopublishing.com

Published by Abdo Publishing, a division of ABDO, PO Box 398166, Minneapolis, Minnesota 55439. Copyright © 2015 by Abdo Consulting Group, Inc. International copyrights reserved in all countries. No part of this book may be reproduced in any form without written permission from the publisher. Core Library™ is a trademark and logo of Abdo Publishing.

Printed in the United States of America, North Mankato, Minnesota
092014
012015

Cover Photo: Mark Allan/Invision/AP Images
Interior Photos: Mark Allan/Invision/AP Images, 1; Bebeto Matthews/AP Images, 4, 45; Mark Lennihan/AP Images, 7; Bettmann/Corbis, 10; Seth Poppel/Yearbook Library, 14; Ted S. Warren/AP Images, 16 (top), 34; Shutterstock Images, 16 (bottom); Veronika Lukasova/ZUMA Wire/Corbis, 18; Doug Wilson/Corbis, 21; Dan Lamont/Corbis, 26; AP Images, 31; Red Line Editorial, 28; Maurizio Gambarini/picture-alliance/dpa/AP Images, 37; Aftab Alam Siddiqui/ AP Images, 40

Editor: Arnold Ringstad
Series Designer: Becky Daum

Library of Congress Control Number: 2014944225

Cataloging-in-Publication Data
Kjelle, Marylou Morano.
  Bill Gates: Microsoft founder and philanthropist / Marylou Morano Kjelle.
     p. cm. -- (Newsmakers)
Includes bibliographical references and index.
ISBN 978-1-62403-641-5
1. Gates, Bill, 1955- --Juvenile literature. 2. Microsoft Corporation--History--Juvenile literature. 3. Computer software industry--United States--Biography--Juvenile literature.
4. Businessmen--United States--Biography--Juvenile literature. 5. Bill & Melinda Gates Foundation--History--Juvenile literature.
  1.Title.
338.7/61004092--dc23
[B]
                                                                        2014944225

CONTENTS

CHAPTER ONE

BACK AT MICROSOFT

n early 2014, Bill Gates made a surprising career move. The 58-year-old billionaire was among the world's wealthiest people. Nearly 40 years earlier, he had founded Microsoft. The software maker became the world's largest technology company. In 2000 he had stepped down as Microsoft's chief executive officer (CEO). He continued to help design the company's software in his position as chief

By the early 2010s, Gates was focusing mostly on his philanthropy.

software architect. In 2008 he left this role to focus on philanthropy. The Bill & Melinda Gates Foundation was formed to work on health care and poverty issues around the world. Gates spent more of his time with the foundation.

In 2014 the computer industry was changing rapidly. Microsoft was finding it difficult to adjust. The company needed to adapt if it was going to remain successful. Gates made a surprising announcement. He would take a more active role in the company he founded. His new title became Technology Advisor. He began developing new products. Gates believed Microsoft's future was bright.

Hardware and Software

A computer is made up of hardware and software. Hardware includes the physical parts of the computer. The mouse, hard drive, and processor are examples of computer hardware. Software programs are the set of instructions the computer follows. Software is sometimes referred to as code, applications, or apps.

Microsoft developed versions of Windows for smartphones and tablets to remain competitive in the modern computer industry.

A Software Pioneer

Gates cofounded Microsoft in 1975 to make computer software. One of his biggest successes was an operating system called Windows. Operating systems let other programs work with the computer's processor and memory. Windows became the world's top operating system.

At one time, Microsoft was the largest technology company in the world. However, in the six years

Cloud Computing

Cloud computing is a general term for accessing information over the Internet. Programs and files can be used from any Internet-connected device. For instance, you could take a photo on a smartphone and upload it to your account using the Internet. When you sign into your account on a computer, you can see the photo you took. Mobile devices often use cloud computing.

Gates was away, the computer industry had changed. Customers were less interested in desktop computers. Most Microsoft software ran on these devices. Mobile devices such as smartphones and tablets became more popular. Gates and Microsoft needed to develop mobile programs and services. The company began developing cloud-computing software to keep up with the industry.

Gates is a technical genius, a hard worker, and a business expert. In the 1980s and 1990s, he used these skills to make computers a part of everyday life. Gates continues to bring technology to people in new and interesting ways.

Computer literacy is the ability to use and understand personal computers (PCs). At an event in 1997, Gates said computer literacy is just as important as the ability to read and write. Gates said:

> Computers are a lot like books when they were first utilized. Initially they are used only by a narrow set of people but to the advantage of everybody—for example, medical researchers. But what you really want is to have a concept of computer literacy like you have for normal literacy. You can achieve this, for example, by providing every library with a PC that is linked to the Internet. As part of your school curriculum, you should be exposed to the Internet.
>
> Source: Janet Lowe. Bill Gates Speaks. New York: Wiley, 1998. Print. 191.

Back It Up

Gates made this comment before the Internet was widely used in libraries and classrooms. Has his vision been achieved today? Write a paragraph answering this question using evidence from Gates's quote and your own personal experience.

CHAPTER TWO

GROWING UP

William Henry Gates III was born on October 28, 1955, in Seattle, Washington. His father, William H. Gates II, was an attorney. His mother, Mary Maxwell Gates, was a schoolteacher. Bill had an older sister named Kristi and a younger sister named Libby.

Gates grew up in Seattle, a booming seaside city.

A Math Genius

As a child, Bill was full of energy. For fun he played sports and board games such as Risk. Bill liked to compete. When he played, he wanted to win. Bill also liked to read. He especially enjoyed science fiction. His favorite authors were Isaac Asimov and Edgar Rice Burroughs. As a child, Bill read encyclopedias from cover to cover.

Science and math were Bill's best subjects in school. He could solve math problems quickly and easily. Bill's parents realized public school was not challenging him. When he was 11 years old, they sent him to Lakeside School. This private school was near his home in Seattle. Bill had a hard time fitting in with others. Classmates teased him because he was so smart. He could also be shy.

It was at Lakeside that Bill first began working with computers. Lakeside did not own its own computer. Instead, it rented a PDP-10 computer. PDP-10s were the size of several refrigerators lined up next to each other. They were primitive by today's standards. But at the time, they were popular in universities and research labs. Bill wrote his first computer program when he was 13 years old. It was a tic-tac-toe game. He used a programming language called BASIC.

Lakeside Programmers

In 1968 Bill formed a club called the Lakeside Programmers Group. A boy named Paul Allen, who was two years ahead of Bill at Lakeside, was also a member. The two became good friends. They spent their free time in the school's computer center. They

BASIC

BASIC stands for Beginner's All-purpose Symbolic Instruction Code. It was invented by two math professors at Dartmouth College in New Hampshire, John Kemeny and Thomas Kurtz. It was first used on May 1, 1964. Like Gates and Allen, the two professors believed computers would play an important role in everyday life. They wanted people to know how to use them. BASIC made computer programming easier than ever before.

Gates, *right*, and Paul Allen, *left*, worked together
during Gates's freshman year.

both believed computers would become a part of everyday life.

The club wanted to find ways to make money with computers. When Bill was in eighth grade, Lakeside began renting PDP-10 computer time from Computer Center Corporation. Bill and his friends referred to the company as "C-Cubed." The PDP-10 computers often crashed, or stopped working. The Lakeside Programmers Group made a deal with C-Cubed. They would find the errors that caused crashes. In return, C-Cubed would give Lakeside all the free computer time it could use. Bill and Paul spent hours at C-Cubed figuring out how to fix the errors. However,

The Evolution of Computers

The top image shows a person programming a PDP-10 computer. The bottom image shows a person using Microsoft's Windows 8 operating system, released in 2012. In what ways has computer technology changed since the 1960s? Use evidence from the images and from Chapter Two.

Bill neglected his schoolwork. His parents worried he was becoming addicted to computers. They made him give up computers for several months.

Bill had other interests, including tennis and reading. But working with computers was what he liked best. This was an exciting time for Bill. Not only was he learning about computers, but he was also becoming an entrepreneur. He started a company called Traf-O-Data with Paul Allen. They wrote a computer program to analyze car traffic patterns. They earned money from selling this information to cities and towns. It was the first of many computer adventures for them.

CHAPTER THREE

WINDOWS OF OPPORTUNITY

n 1973 Gates graduated from Lakeside. He enrolled at Harvard University in Cambridge, Massachusetts. Paul Allen was working for an electronics firm near Harvard.

In 1975 Micro Instrumentation and Telemetry Systems (MITS) released the Altair 8800. It was one of the earliest home computers. However, buyers did not receive a fully functional, assembled device.

The Altair 8800 lacked many features of modern computers, including a screen and a keyboard.

The Altair 8800 came as a kit. Users had to put it together themselves. It had limited memory. It also lacked a screen and keyboard. Users programmed the computer using switches on its front panel. Despite these shortcomings, many computer users were excited about the Altair.

Starting Microsoft

The Altair had another problem. It had no way to use a simple programming language, such as BASIC. Gates and Allen were sure they could write a program to make this possible. They contacted MITS and claimed to have a BASIC program for the Altair. Gates and Allen suggested that MITS sell their BASIC program with the Altair. In return, Gates and Allen wanted money for each computer sold.

However, Gates and Allen hadn't yet written the BASIC program. Now they had to get it done. Gates stopped going to his classes at Harvard. He and Allen worked almost nonstop for five weeks. In late February 1975, Allen traveled to MITS in

Allen, *left*, and Gates, *right*, were able to back up their bluff with impressive programming skills.

Albuquerque, New Mexico, to test BASIC on the Altair. The program worked. Allen began working at MITS.

Gates finished his sophomore year at Harvard. He then joined Allen in Albuquerque. That summer Gates and Allen formed a software company. They called it Micro-Soft, short for "microcomputer software." The name was soon shortened to "Microsoft." Microsoft's first project was getting the bugs out of the Altair

BASIC program. Gates hired two former schoolmates to help. The four worked seven days a week. They stopped only to sleep and eat. Their plan was to write BASIC for other computers. Microsoft would license its software to more computer companies.

The Altair 8800 started a computer craze. Within five years, almost 200 different personal computers flooded the market. Apple, Commodore, and Tandy became the leaders in the personal computer industry. Thousands of computers were sold daily. Each needed applications, a programming language, and an operating system. Gates decided that Microsoft could provide all three.

In January 1977 Gates left Harvard to become the CEO of Microsoft. He never returned to finish his degree. Two years later, Gates and Allen moved Microsoft to Bellevue, Washington.

Working with IBM

International Business Machines (IBM) was a well-known company that wanted to get into the personal computer business. Instead of making its own computers, however, IBM wanted to build them from parts made by other companies. In 1980 Microsoft agreed to partner with IBM. It would develop the software and operating system for IBM's personal computer.

Gates paid $50,000 to Seattle Computer Products for their Quick and Dirty Operating System (QDOS). Gates made changes to it and renamed it the Microsoft Disk Operating System (MS-DOS). IBM called the operating system PC-DOS.

Paul Allen

In 1983 Paul Allen was diagnosed with Hodgkin's disease, a type of cancer. Allen left Microsoft to focus on treatment. He remained on the company's board of directors. The treatments were successful. His cancer went into remission. Allen has started several companies over the years. Many are related to cable television and the Internet. Allen also owns the NBA's Portland Trailblazers and the NFL's Seattle Seahawks. Like Gates, Allen is a philanthropist. He has donated money to medical research, the arts, and forest preservation.

Windows

MS-DOS was difficult to use because it required the user to type commands on a keyboard. These were followed by responses on the screen. Later versions of MS-DOS allowed people to use other devices, such as printers. In 1985 Microsoft released Windows 1.0. This program ran alongside DOS. Users controlled a mouse to point and click on icons representing files and folders. In 1995 Microsoft released Windows 95. The operating system is one of the most successful software products of all time. In 2014 most computers in the world still used a version of the Windows operating system.

IBM released its personal computer in 1981. It was extremely successful. Other companies wanted their computers to be compatible with IBM's machines. Microsoft licensed its software to these other manufacturers. Then, in the mid-1980s, Microsoft began developing new applications. Applications are programs that do specific tasks. For example, word processors and games are applications. Microsoft grew to become a leader in applications.

Throughout the 1980s, Microsoft maintained its leadership in the computer industry. Gates and Allen became billionaires.

CHAPTER FOUR

MICROSOFT IN TROUBLE

Microsoft enjoyed success, but it also had its share of trouble. In 1988 Apple Computer sued Microsoft for copyright violation. Apple believed Windows looked and worked a lot like its Macintosh operating system. The company accused Microsoft of stealing Apple's design. The court case was dismissed in 1993. Microsoft continued to develop and sell Windows.

Gates vigorously defended Microsoft when the company encountered legal trouble.

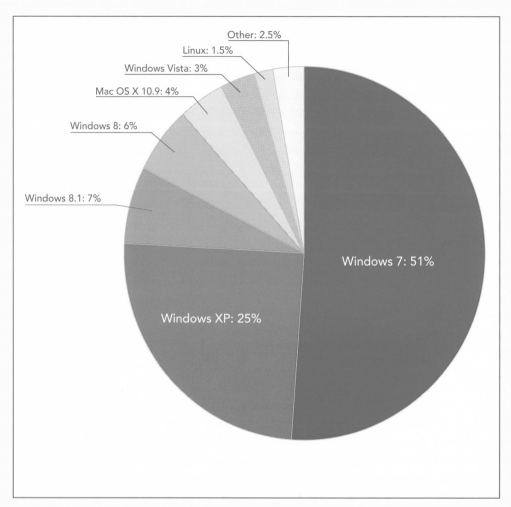

Other: 2.5%
Linux: 1.5%
Windows Vista: 3%
Mac OS X 10.9: 4%
Windows 8: 6%
Windows 8.1: 7%
Windows 7: 51%
Windows XP: 25%

Microsoft's Market Share

Microsoft still dominates the operating system market today. This graph shows roughly what percentage of computer users ran each major operating system in July 2014. What do you notice about Microsoft's market share? How does this graph demonstrate Microsoft's influence in the personal computer industry?

Investigating Microsoft

Around the same time, the Federal Trade Commission (FTC), a government agency that regulates businesses, began investigating Microsoft. It looked into claims that Microsoft's business practices discouraged competition. Microsoft required computer makers to pay a fee for its operating system, even if the computer used a different operating system. Because of this, most manufacturers installed Windows, since they had to pay Microsoft anyway. The FTC claimed this forced people to use Microsoft software. The matter was settled in 1994. Microsoft agreed to stop requiring this licensing.

The Internet also brought trouble for Microsoft. Users need a Web browser program to view websites on the Internet. Netscape Navigator was the dominant Web browser in the early 1990s. In 1995 Microsoft released its own Web browser, Internet Explorer. The company packaged it with Windows. In 1998 Netscape and other Microsoft competitors

Microsoft Saves Apple

Another big computer name to emerge in the 1980s was Apple. Microsoft created a word processor for Apple's Macintosh computer. However, once Microsoft developed Windows, it began competing with Apple's own operating system. By the mid-1990s, Microsoft dominated the personal computer industry. Apple was on the verge of bankruptcy. In 1997 Microsoft stepped in and invested $150 million into Apple. Microsoft's money helped Apple stay in business. After an incredible comeback, Apple became a larger company than Microsoft in 2010.

accused Microsoft of unfairly dominating the Internet browser market. They claimed that by including Internet Explorer with Windows, Microsoft was forcing anyone who purchased Windows to purchase Internet Explorer as well. In 1997 a judge ruled that Microsoft had to separate its Windows software from Internet Explorer. However, the ruling was overturned in 1998. Microsoft continued to release Windows with Internet Explorer.

Microsoft has continued to bundle new versions of Internet Explorer alongside Windows.

Another Federal Investigation

The United States government continued investigating Microsoft. In a 1998 lawsuit, the US Justice Department said Microsoft was using anticompetitive business practices. Once again

Gates as CEO

In the early days of Microsoft, Allen spent most of his time programming. Gates wrote programming code too, but he also took care of sales and marketing. Gates was an unusual businessman. For one thing, he was only 19 years old when he founded the company. On most days he wore jeans to work. His hair was long and unruly. He rocked back and forth when he was trying to make a decision. To many people, Gates looked like a college kid with a summer job. However, this impression vanished when Gates began to talk business. He was aggressive and highly protective of Microsoft and its software.

Microsoft was accused of forcing people to purchase Internet Explorer. The government said this hurt both Microsoft's competition and computer users. It made people purchase software they might not want. Microsoft denied the charges. It claimed it had acted fairly. Gates did not appear in the courtroom, but lawyers interviewed him. A video of the interview was shown at the trial. In it he strongly defended Microsoft.

In 2000 a judge ruled that Microsoft had acted unfairly by bundling its browser and operating system. The company was ordered to split in two. One company would sell Windows. The other would sell Microsoft software. Microsoft appealed the ruling. In 2001 the case was settled. Microsoft would stay intact. It could continue developing both Windows and Internet Explorer.

EXPLORE ONLINE

Chapter Four talks about Microsoft's Windows operating system. You may have used a version of Windows at home or school. The website below provides more information about the history of the operating system. It shows images from each version, going back to Windows 1.0. How much has changed in the past several decades? How is the information in this timeline different from the information in this chapter? How do the two sources present information differently?

History of Windows
www.mycorelibrary.com/bill-gates

A COMPASSIONATE BILLIONAIRE

Bill Gates stepped down as the CEO of Microsoft in 2000. Steve Ballmer replaced him. Ballmer had been an employee of Microsoft since 1980. He was known for his energetic personality. Gates stayed at the company in the position of chief software architect. He preferred to focus on the company's products rather than running the business.

Ballmer, left, went on to serve as Microsoft CEO for 14 years.

The Giving Pledge

Bill Gates and billionaire investor Warren Buffett are both passionate about philanthropy. Both are trying to get more of the world's billionaires to take an active role in helping the poor. In 2010 they announced the Giving Pledge. So far more than 100 billionaires across the world have pledged to donate at least half of their wealth to charity. The Giving Pledge brings additional money to programs that help people in need. It also makes people more aware of suffering throughout the world.

The Gates Foundation

In the early 2000s, Gates began devoting more time to philanthropy. In 2000 he and his wife, Melinda, formed the Bill & Melinda Gates Foundation. They have since donated more than $28 billion to the foundation. The organization helps people throughout the world deal with hunger, poverty, and disease. Its missions are diverse. The foundation works to eliminate malaria in Africa. It helps farmers grow crops in South Asia. It improves education in the United States. The

Gates has met with world leaders, including German chancellor Angela Merkel, to discuss philanthropy.

Melinda Gates

Melinda Ann French was born in Dallas, Texas, on August 15, 1964. She graduated from Duke University with degrees in computer science and business. She began working as a product manager at Microsoft in 1987. Melinda met Gates at a trade show. The couple dated for six years before marrying in 1994. They have three children: Jennifer, Rory, and Phoebe. Melinda left Microsoft in 1996. After her departure, she focused on nonprofit organizations and charities, including the Gates Foundation. She is especially interested in making sure women in developing countries have access to contraception, giving them choices about whether to have children.

foundation has given away more than $20 billion since 2000.

In 2006 Gates prepared to stop working at Microsoft full time. He wanted to spend more time with the foundation. On June 27, 2008, Gates worked his last full day at Microsoft. Six years later, in 2014, he returned to Microsoft to advise the company.

Gates had spent years helping to distribute vaccines and save lives around the world. His foundation has focused on simple ways to make big changes in the lives of the poor. For example, it launched a program to design inexpensive toilets that do not require running water or electricity. The program sought to improve sanitation for the world's poorest citizens. However, Gates retained his intense passion for technology.

Changing the World

With an estimated worth of approximately $76 billion, Gates was the richest person in the world in 2014. Gates used intelligence and determination to start Microsoft. He brought about a computer revolution that changed the world. Though Gates is back at Microsoft now, he continues to put major effort into his foundation. He and Melinda often visit the countries where the foundation works. Gates believes their foundation and others like it can change the world.

The issues facing the world's billions of poor, sick, and hungry people are immense. But Gates has never been one to shrink from a challenge. As an

Gates, right, and Melinda, *left*, sometimes meet with the communities they help.

entrepreneur, business leader, and philanthropist, Bill Gates has made his mark on the world. Now the man who made Microsoft one of the most successful companies in history is improving the lives of people everywhere.

Each year, Gates writes a letter to supporters of the Gates Foundation to update them on progress toward the foundation's goals. He also outlines his vision for the future of the foundation. In his 2014 letter, Gates wrote:

> Africa has also made big strides in health and education. Since 1960, the life span for women in sub-Saharan Africa has gone up from 41 to 57 years, despite the HIV epidemic. Without HIV it would be 61 years. The percentage of children in school has gone from the low 40s to over 75 percent since 1970. Fewer people are hungry, and more people have good nutrition. If getting enough to eat, going to school, and living longer are measures of a good life, then life is definitely getting better there. These improvements are not the end of the story; they're the foundation for more progress.
>
> Source: Bill Gates. "2014 Annual Gates Letter." Gates Foundation. Gates Foundation, January 2014. Web. Accessed July 31, 2014.

What's the Big Idea?

In his letter, Gates discusses the progress that has been made in Africa. How does Gates make his point using statistics? Why might he be interested in using statistics to mark progress? Do you find his point convincing?

IMPORTANT DATES

1955

William Henry Gates III is born in Seattle, Washington.

1968

The Lakeside Programmers Group is formed.

1975

Gates and Paul Allen write a BASIC program for the Altair.

1997

Microsoft invests $150 million in Apple.

1998

The US Department of Justice files a lawsuit against Microsoft.

2000

Gates and his wife, Melinda, form the Bill & Melinda Gates Foundation.

1981

Microsoft works with IBM to develop software for the IBM computer.

1985

Microsoft introduces Windows.

1994

Gates marries Melinda French.

2008

Gates gives up his day-to-day role at Microsoft to spend more time on the Bill & Melinda Gates Foundation.

2010

Gates announces the Giving Pledge campaign.

2014

Gates returns to an active role at Microsoft.

Why Do I Care?

This book discusses the beginnings of the personal computer market in the 1970s. At that time, computers did not use graphical user interfaces. Instead many simply showed text on the screen. Some used only blinking lights. Do you think you would be able to use one of these early computers? Do you rely on modern graphical user interfaces when using computers today?

Take a Stand

This book talks about how Microsoft helped Apple when Apple had financial problems. Today, the two companies continue to develop rival operating systems. Apple is now a larger company than Microsoft. Should Gates and Microsoft have stepped in to help Apple in 1997? Write a short essay explaining your opinion. Make sure you give reasons for your opinion, and facts and details that support those reasons.

Say What?

The computer field contains a huge number of technical terms. Find five words in this book that you've never heard before. Use a dictionary to find out what they mean. Write the meanings in your own words, and use each word in a new sentence.

Tell the Tale

Chapter Five talks about Gates's commitment to helping people in need. Write a story about a person who is helped by the Gates Foundation. People in the United States often think of Bill Gates as a billionaire computer company executive. How might people in poverty think of him?

GLOSSARY

bankruptcy
the legal status of having little or no money

board of directors
a group of people who provide advice to a company's leaders

chief executive officer (CEO)
the leader of a company

copyright
the legal right to reproduce or sell an invention or published work

entrepreneur
one who takes a risk in starting a new business

foundation
an organization that gives money to charities

license
to allow others to use a product in exchange for money

operating system
the program on a computer that allows other programs to run

philanthropy
giving away money to charitable causes

LEARN MORE

Books

DeMuth, Patricia Brennan. *Who is Bill Gates?* New York: Grosset & Dunlap, 2013.

Gregory, Josh. *Bill and Melinda Gates.* New York: Children's Press, 2013.

Websites

To learn more about Newsmakers, visit **booklinks.abdopublishing.com**. These links are routinely monitored and updated to provide the most current information available.

Visit **www.mycorelibrary.com** for free additional tools for teachers and students.

INDEX

ABOUT THE AUTHOR

Marylou Morano Kjelle is a college English professor, a
freelance writer, and the author of more than 50 books
for young people. Many of the books she has written are
biographies.